NEW ORLEANS

100 Color illustrations

Text by
ROSANNA CIRIGLIANO

Photographic service by
ANDREA PISTOLESI

FB
BONECHI

Distribution by

EXPRESS PUBLISHING CO.
305 DECATUR STREET
NEW ORLEANS, LOUISIANA 70130

Phone: 504-524-6963/504-524-2604

We thank
Beverly Gianna, Greater
New Orleans Tourist
and Convention Commission
for the help in
compiling this book.

© Copyright 1989 by
CASA EDITRICE BONECHI
Via Cairoli 18/b
50131 Firenze - Italia
Telex 571323 CEB
Fax 55-576844

Printed in E.E.C. by
Centro Stampa Editoriale Bonechi

The spirit underlying New Orleans is pure jazz. The heart of jazz is improvisation; the musician takes a basic idea and changes it to fit his style of playing, much in the manner of this city, its birthplace. Jazz is a blending of various influences, hot, sassy and throbbing with life. Something new and uniquely American was created in both cases, with European, African and Caribbean overtones.

Jazz is freshly invented with every performance, and that accounts for much of its vitality. Similarly, the history of New Orleans is full of unexpected twists, which have given the city its character.

BETWEEN THE DEVIL AND THE DEEP BLUE SEA

The first Europeans to venture to the lower Mississippi valley were the fearless Spanish explorers Cabeza de Vaca and Panfilo de Narvaez in 1530. More than a century later Frenchman Robert Cavalier, Sieur de La Salle, traced the entire length of the Mississippi River, claiming the contingent area (827,192 square miles, out of which 17 states were carved in whole or in part) for his homeland in 1682.

He christened the vast expanse "Louisane", in honor of Louis XIV, the Sun King. A Scot, John Law, entered the scene in 1717, having obtained a charter to exploit the Louisiana Territory with the aid of Philippe d'Orléans, regent to Louis XV. Law in turn sent another Frenchman, Jean-Baptiste le Moyne, Sieur de Bienville, to establish a settlement. De Bienville selected a location on the east bank of the river, 110 miles from the Gulf, building a tiny outpost on low-lying land which he named in 1718 "Nouvelle Orléans".

What was later known simply as "New Orleans" became capital of the entire territory in 1722. Its inhabitants exported tobacco, indigo and naval supplies; however, since the value of such cargo at that time did not match its bulk, French ships were reluctant to call at New Orleans. So, France parted with its unprofitable port and the Louisiana Territory west of the Mississippi to Spain in 1763, under the terms of the Treaty of Paris. Spain maintained control of the area up to 1800, when it was secretly returned to France. Distrusting and fearing Napoleon, Thomas Jefferson instructed his minister in Paris, Robert Livingston, to negotiate for the purchase of New Orleans. But Napoleon did not decide to sell the city until 1803, when news arrived that a French expeditionary force in the Mississippi Valley had been wiped out by a combination of yellow fever

and bad weather. He threw the entire Louisiana Territory into the bargain, for the purchase price of $15 million, one of the best deals the United States was ever to make.

New Orleans was incorporated as a city in 1805, and Louisiana became the 18th state to enter the Union, in 1812.

THAT'S MY HOME

The early inhabitants of New Orleans were a lively mix of rough Canadian frontiersmen, artisans and troops from John Law's Company of the West (which ruled the area until it reverted back to a French crown colony in 1731), convicts and black and Indian slaves. In 1727 some 88 women freed from Parisian prisons arrived to become the colony's first brides, chaperoned by eight Ursuline nuns. The intrepid nuns established themselves on what is now Chartres Street; they had a convent designed and built further down the same street. Begun in 1745, this edifice near today's French Market is the only one in New Orleans surviving from the period of French domination.

Adventure-loving and opportunity-seeking Frenchmen and other Europeans soon followed in the footsteps of the original settlers. The word *Creole*, coined and used in the French West Indies, was carried over to Louisiana to indicate a person born there of pure French blood. The derivation and concept came from the Spanish term *criollo*, which distinguished the first generation in the New World born of Spanish parents. Later, it referred to the proud descendants of the first settlers, in many cases of mixed French and Spanish origin.

The Spanish did not turn up in New Orleans until 1766, a full four years after ascending to power. After effectively quelling a revolt they quietly

3

Skyscrapers in the background of New Orleans.

Right, *aerial views of Jackson Square, heart of the French Quarter, with skyscrapers of the modern city in the background.*

settled down to leaving their imprint on the city's architecture and way of life. Around the same period a group later called "the Cajuns" made its way to New Orleans. They were the descendants of French colonists who had settled in Arcadia, later the Canadian province of Nova Scotia. The British took command of the region by force in 1715, inaugurating an era of strife between the Protestant rulers and the Catholic population. The British finally expelled the "Cadians" in 1755; some returned to France, others made their way down to Louisiana. The Spanish later arranged to bring to New Orleans several thousands of those exiles who had gone back to France. The Cajuns' inimitable zest for living would soon be absorbed into the local culture.

The "Americans" came next. During the Revolutionary War, the "Kaintucks" (not necessarily from Kentucky, but those who went downriver on a raft and back again) began floating cargo to New Orleans. The Spanish rulers had to suspend their use of the port on more than one occasion because of their rowdiness. Undeterred, they came in greater numbers by river and also on foot down the Natchez Trace, to trade and to live in New Orleans.

Many of these "Kaintucks" were Celts, that is Scots-Irish, and their presence was not initially looked upon in a kind manner by the aristocratic Creoles. So they settled across from the French Quarter. The land dividing the two sections was intended to be a drainage canal; it was made into a wide boulevard with a median down the center nicknamed "neutral ground". Natives still call any median "neutral ground".

Let's not forget that the great wave of European immigration to the U.S. from the mid-nineteenth to the early twentieth centuries would bring native Germans, Irish and Italians to New Orleans. The African-American heritage is also a deep-rooted and intense one. Before the Civil War, "free men of color" were musicians, journalists, poets, businessmen and landlords. Blacks earned a fine reputation for their artistry and workmanship in the fields of iron grillework and carpentry. New Orleans is one place in the country where the black contribution to local culture is clearly distinct.

4

When New Orleans was the Capital of the Spanish Province of Luisiana. 1762 – 1803 This square bore the name PLAZA ꝺ ARMAS

Above, *sign detailing the historic background of Jackson Square. Below, street artists displaying their work are a common sight in the Square.*

Aerial view of Jackson Square.

I AIN'T GONNA PLAY NO SECOND FIDDLE

Designed along the lines of a typical French village by engineer Adrian de Pauger in 1721, the **Vieux Carré** or **French Quarter** is the living soul of a jazzy city, where characteristic buildings manifest clear French, Spanish and American influences. **Jackson Square** is at the very center of the Vieux Carré's grid layout. Facing the river, the square is a haven of greenery, shrubs and trees which reflects a very human blending of city history and contemporary life. An aerial view provides a counterpoint by showing a backdrop of modern New Orleans and its skyscrapers.
It is clear from Jackson Square that authority in the form of the Roman Catholic Church and civil government constituted the backbone of the original colony. At that time the square was simply a parade field known as the *Place d'Armes* (literally: Weapons Square). Soldiers drilled in front of the town church (known several versions later as the St. Louis Cathedral), successively flanked by the headquarters of the Spanish town council (the Cabildo) as well as a proposed residence for the clergy (the Presbytère). After inheriting the common, the Spanish adapted the name to *Plaza de Armas*; the Americans were to dub it *Public Square*.
The designation *Jackson Square* was agreed upon in the mid-nineteenth century around the time when an equestrian statue of Andrew Jackson, hero of the battle of New Orleans, was unveiled in the middle.
The square has always attracted people: natives, tourists, artists who exhibit their work on the outside of the cast-iron fence designed by Louis H. Pilé and erected in 1851, drivers with their old-fashioned horse-drawn carriages, musicians

7

The oldest and most important church in New Orleans is the St. Louis Cathedral. Right, note the Cabildo, former headquarters of the Spanish Colonial government to the left of the Cathedral.

who occasionally give impromptu concerts. Nearly everyone gravitates towards the tall-steepled **St. Louis Cathedral**, and the church's impassive white façade calmly surveys the changing scene.

Since the early 1720s there has always been a church on this site, and the present cathedral is the third such structure. The first modest house of worship, carried away by the hurricane of 1722, was named by the initial settlers for King Louis IX, patron saint of France. The second edifice was destroyed in the great fire of 1788, which leveled

much of the old city. The Governor of New Orleans, Don Andrés Almonester y Roxas, a wealthy Spanish nobleman, financed the construction of the new religious building designed by Gilberto Guillemard. Completed in 1794, it managed to emerge unscathed from another massive fire which broke out shortly thereafter to be consecrated a cathedral on Christmas Eve of the same year. Throughout its history, official announcements were posted on the door, much in the tradition of a European church.

Interiors of the St. Louis Cathedral. The altar was made in Belgium.

H.S. Bonval Latrobe made some architectural changes in the church's façade in 1814, and later still, in 1849-51, the St. Louis Cathedral was enlarged on the specifications of architect J.N.B. Pouilly, who also gave it a French appearance by elevating the steeples and adding other remodelling touches.

The interior is graced by painted ceilings and a plain, yet exquisite central altar made in Belgium, Several generations of New Orleans families are buried here, and their tombs bear inscriptions in either French, Spanish, English or Latin. Pope Paul VI elevated the cathedral to the status of a minor basilica in 1964.

MAJOR GENERAL
ANDREW JACKSON

The bronze statue of Andrew Jackson stands at the very center of the square which bears his name. Jackson successfully defended New Orleans from a British invasion force in 1815.

Directly in front of the St. Louis Cathedral is the aforementioned **statue of Andrew Jackson** on horseback, work of sculptor Clark Mills. An outstanding military figure, he is commemorated for saving New Orleans during the War of 1812 from a British invasion force. Jackson and a band of backwoodsmen and local volunteers defeated the enemy on January 8, 1815 outside the city at the Chalmette. Unknown to both sides, a peace treaty ending the war had been signed in Europe two weeks earlier.

The buildings on either side of the Cathedral are symbols of temporal and religious power rather than military might. From the statue of Andrew Jackson you see the Cabildo on the left and the Presbytère on the right. Both are Spanish colonial buildings with French mansard roofs (the Cabildo was built in 1795 to replace an edifice which housed a *corps de garde* – police station – lost in the fire of 1788; the Presbytère was begun during the 1790s). The Cabildo was once the seat of government for the entire Mississippi valley, and the Louisiana Purchase papers were signed there in 1803 on the second floor. Part of the old police station can be seen in the ground floor rooms, and the prison around the back was in use up to 1914. The structure was also the City Hall of New Orleans from 1803 to 1853 and subsequently housed the Supreme Court of Louisiana (1853-1910). Along with the Presbytère (which was never used as church rectory), the Cabildo is now part of the Louisiana State Museum, which contains many interesting exhibits, including a death mask of Napoleon Bonaparte.

Above left, *a close-up of the French mansard roof of the Cabildo; below left, the twin brick structures known as the Pontalba Apartments are believed to be the first apartment buildings in the U.S.*

The Jackson Brewery building on the riverfront has been converted into a festive marketplace.

Part of the same museum is a section of the **Lower Pontalba Building**, on the Ann Street side of Jackson Square. Like its twin directly opposite, the **Upper Pontalba Building** (a situation that reminds you of piazza Santissima Annunziata in Florence, Italy) the structure was designed in red brick around 1850 with long sweeping balconies enclosed by delicate cast-iron grillework. Made in France, the pattern of the open grillework contains the initials "A P" for Micaela Almonester, Baroness de Pontealba, daughter of Don Andrés Almonester y Roxas (see St. Louis Cathedral), who commissioned the buildings to architects James Gallier Sr. and Henry Howard. As intended, they are a complex of graceful ground floor shops and private residences above; the part belonging to the Louisiana State Museum faithfully re-creates the atmosphere of a mid-nineteenth century New Orleans dwelling, complete with period furniture. A modern shopping experience can be had at the nearby **Jackson Brewery** at 620 Decatur Street. The former brewery site was converted into a spectacular multi-level upscale festive marketplace during the 1980s and features over 100 modern shops and boutiques plus food stands and restaurants. A pleasant way to relax after browsing around could be to order a drink at one of the JAX's (as it is affectionately known) roof-top terrace lounges and admire a panorama of the city and the Mississippi river.

TOO MARVELOUS FOR WORDS

Close your eyes in New Orleans, and invariably you hear music playing. The smokey sound of jazz is all around, with individual musicians improvising on the streets of the French Quarter or the river, rhythms exploding at Mardi Gras celebrations, and a brass marching band providing an upbeat final exit at the funeral of a friend.

Louis Armstrong, Buddy Bolden, Jelly Roll Morton, Duke Ellington, Count Basie, Charlie Parker and Dizzy Gillespie are but a few of the greats who come to mind on the theme of jazz. This art form was born in New Orleans shortly before the First World War. It derived from a background of ragtime, blues, Scots-Irish fiddlers' tunes, old Louisiana Creole dance tunes, spirituals, revival hymns and black work songs. Jazz always has a bounce or swing because it is syncopated music. Put together a trumpet, trombone, sax, clarinet, bass and drums, and you've got the basic components of a jazz band. Add the players, and

Bourbon Street is the place to go for evening entertainment.

17

On the left, *Pat O'Brien's is a New Orleans landmark.*

The French Market's Café du Monde is open 24 hours a day for café au lait *and* beignets *(French donuts).*

what happens next is anyone's guess. Or, according to an old New Orleans saying, "Let the good times roll!"

The excitement of this New Orleans tradition continues unabated on the Vieux Carré's **Bourbon Street**, where jazz is served up fresh night and day, day and night. Two renowned jazz musicians have their own clubs there, Al Hirt and Pete Fountain. The numerous jazz joints in the area flow with pure creative energy, sound and liquor. For those interested in a combination of soft music and hard drink, a good bet is **Pat O'Brien's** on nearby St. Peter Street. The establishment has three bars: the Main Bar, one in the beautifully spacious Patio, and another in the Cocktail Lounge, where pianists and singers entertain the crowd nightly from 8 pm to 4 am. The place is famous for its Hurricane drink, served in a 29 oz. handblown crested glass, which is in great demand as a souvenir of Pat O'Brien's and New Orleans.

At a certain point coffee is needed. This provides an opportunity to take a stroll, or a carriage ride through the French Quarter down to the river and the Café du Monde at the end of the French Market. Like Bourbon Street, the **Café du Monde** never sleeps – you can ask any time for *café au lait*, strong chicory-flavored coffee and hot milk, and a *beignet*, a square-shaped donut minus the hole, dusted with powdered sugar.

*The French Market is a delightful place along
the Mississippi River.*

After completing your purchases, take a rest in this characteristic park close to the French Market.

A relaxing way to take in the sights of the French Quarter is to take an old-fashioned carriage ride.

Let that be your introduction to the cuisine of New Orleans, probably the most exciting in the United States. The raw ingredients are often the local seafood, rice, beans, chicken, pork, vegetables and spices, all stirred into something magnificent on the basis of Cajun and Creole recipes. Cajun dishes basically reflect a robust, fairly hot country style of cooking, while "city" Creole food is spicier, and characterized by the use of sauces. Some local specialities include *crawfish étoufée* and *shrimp étoufée* (seafood cooked in a tomato-based, sauce), *gumbo filé* (a thick soup of shrimp, crab meat, okra, aromatic herbs and rice), *jambalaya* (a potful of saffron rice, tomatoes, ham, shrimp, chicken, celery, onions and spices),

red beans and rice (plus hunks of sausage meat, usually eaten on Monday), and *blackened redfish*. Not to forget French specialities like raw oysters on the half shell, roast veal and duck, trout covered in meuniere sauce. And of course *pralines*, that is, pecan candy.
These dishes may be ordered in elegant restaurants, or made at home with the help of a book on Louisiana cooking by somebody like Paul Prudhomme. A kitchenful of ingredients can be purchased at the nearby **French Market** on the riverfront not far from Jackson Square. Natives have done their shopping there for over the past 150 years. Open-air stalls are piled high with fruits and vegetables grown on local truck farms,

Above left, an example of the eclectic architecture characteristic of New Orleans, below left, the city is especially renowned for its open iron grillework balconies.

A row of open iron grillework balconies offers a stunning sight.

and a variety of meats, fowl, flounder, snapper, channel catfish and blue crabs crowd the counters. For those not particularly interested in food, the French Market also offers craft often located under arcades in a setting reminiscent of the Old World.

New Orleans is also a feast for the eye. The cityscape reflects a myriad architectural styles: modern skyscrapers, graceful Italianate mansions and gardens, sturdy American townhouses, classic Greek Revival structures, and fascinating Victorian houses enlivened with such Gothic Revival details as pointed arches. But it is the French and Spanish colonial refinement of the Vieux Carré which remains the main sightseeing

delight.

The older homes in the Vieux Carré are constructed of a heavy timber framework filled with brickwork, and plastered over. This technique used by French builders in Louisiana known as *briquette entre poteaux,* "brick between the posts", can be seen in an eighteenth century cottage, now a bar, at 941 Bourbon Street. The structure is known as **Lafitte's Blacksmith Shop,** although no evidence exists to connect it with the famed pirate. This one-story cottage placed directly on the sidewalk is typical of the 1700s, distinguished by windows reaching to the ground and a high-pitched roof.

Another kind of Creole house is an L-shaped,

25

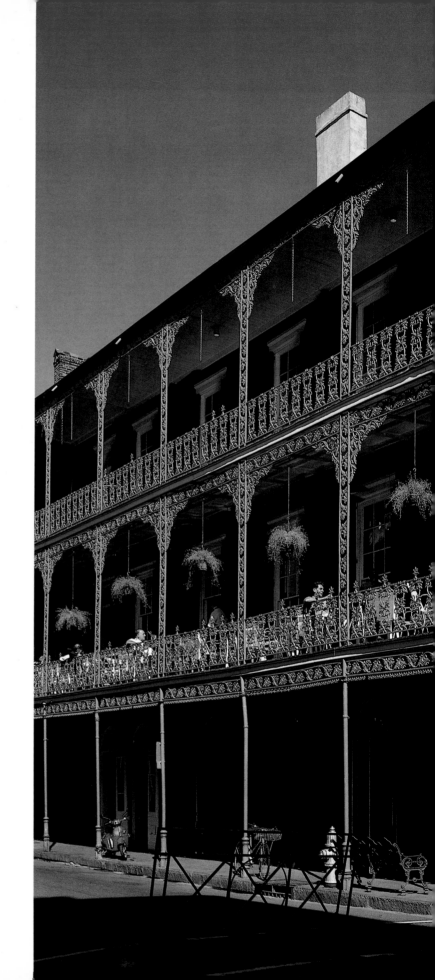

The La Branche building with its
fabulous cast-iron galleries is perhaps
one of the best known structures in
the Vieux Carré.

On these pages the open iron grillework you see was the product of local craftsmanship in the 19th century.

two-story dwelling again placed right on the sidewalk, and attached to similar buildings with no space between them. A side entrance usually provides access to the trees, flowers, and fountains of an inner patio. An especially beautiful example of this private space is the Brulatour Courtyard, part of the early nineteenth century François Seignouret House at 520 Royal Street, now home to the WDSU TV station.

But perhaps the image that remains most in the visitor's mind of the Vieux Carré is one of terraces and hanging plants.

These range from simple balconies in wrought iron supported underneath by brackets, to elaborate galleries of cast iron which extend entirely around a building.

The latter can almost look like a wedding cake, tier upon tier of intricate swirls held up by colonettes. The **La Branche Building** at 700 Royal Street is probably the most stunning structure of this type in New Orleans. Commissioned in 1840 by Melasie Trepagnier La Branche, widow of Jean Baptiste La Branche, the cast-iron galleries feature a well-ordered pattern of oak leaves and acorns. Part of the distinctive architecture too are wooden street signs, often hand-carved and hand-painted, advertising art galleries, antique shops, perfume shops, tea rooms and cafés. The *ambiance* around Royal Street is a little like that of Paris's Left Bank.

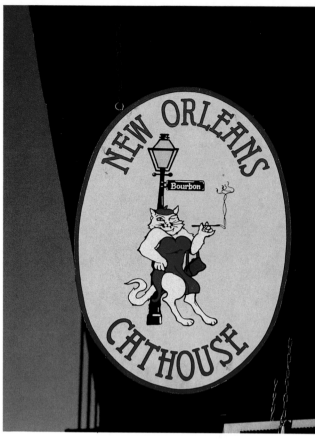

Some of the hand-carved and hand-painted signs of the Vieux Carré.

BODY AND SOUL

The past is very much present in today's New Orleans. This can be seen in the private residences of a bygone era open to the public. One is the **Hermann-Grima House** on 820 St. Louis Street, still in the Vieux Carré, which stands as a singular American contribution to New Orleans architecture. Built in 1831 for Samuel Hermann Sr., it is made of Philadelphia brick in a modified Georgian style then prevalent along the Eastern seabord. The house changed hands in 1844, passing to Felix Grima, lawyer and notary public. The property remained in the Grima family until 1924, when it was purchased by the Christian Woman's Exchange and turned into a museum. The Hermann-Grima House contains a working 1830s Creole kitchen, and cooking demonstrations are held on the open hearth from October to May by reservation. The rooms are decorated with the sumptuous antique furniture of the period, including a four-poster canopied bed. A restored private stable is located on the grounds as well.

A contrast to the Hermann-Grima House is

Right, *the Hermann-Grima Historical House.* Below, *cooking demonstrations are still given at the house's open hearth.*

The Beauregard-Keyes House is an outstanding example of raised Louisiana cottage style architecture combined with a Greek revival style. Above right, *the house's garden,* below *a glimpse of the bedroom.*

provided by the **Le Carpentier-Beauregard-Keyes House** at 1113 Chartres Street. The house is a fascinating mélange of a raised Louisiana cottage style, French windows, shutters, dormer roof and all, and a Greek Revival style.
There is a courtyard and restored French formal garden. Joseph Le Carpentier, auctioneer and grandfather of chess master Paul Morphy, had this handsome residence built in 1826. Confederate

general P.G.T.
Beauregard lived here for a short while after the end of the Civil War, and novelist Frances Parkinson Keyes made her home here from the Second World War up to her death in 1970. The Keyes Foundation maintains the house as a public museum which safeguards antique furniture, Keyes memorabilia, and a collection of dolls.
A more tangible memorial to the hero

Above, and right, *interiors of the Beauregard-Keyes house re-create the atmosphere of an era gone by.*

Beauregard exists in the form of an **equestrian statue** at the entrance of **City Park**. Some 1500 acres located outside the Vieux Carré and halfway to Lake Pontchartrain provide open space for walking, bicycling, tennis and golf. Water enthusiasts can boat or go fishing in numerous lagoons shaded by 800 year-old oak trees, and children flock to carnival rides and the miniature train.

For culture enthusiasts, the **New Orleans Museum of Art** is also located here in an attractive neoclassical edifice. The museum's collections include works from the Italian Renaissance, pre-Columbian art, African sculptures and French Impressionist masterpieces. Surprisingly enough, another tourist attraction in New Orleans are the cemeteries. As the average elevation of the city is five feet below sea level, underground burials are rendered impossible. This fact prompted the natives to create enclaves known as "cities of the dead" where their loved ones are deposited in above-ground tombs of various architectural styles.

The crypts resemble small rowhouses or Greek-inspired temples, and are made of such materials as marble, brick and stucco. Earlier

35

ones are modest, while those built from 1830 onwards tend to be ornate reproductions of their large-scale counterparts, reflecting a glory of Greek-revival pediments, porticoes and cast-iron grillework. The historic cemeteries are scattered throughout metropolitan New Orleans; their location documents the area's growth since each was situated at the time near or beyond city limits. **St. Louis Cemetery Number One** at 400 Basin Street just outside the Vieux Carré is the oldest and most visited of them all since it tells so much about the city's past. Among the famous people buried there are Etienne de Boré, first mayor of New Orleans, and Marie Laveau, known in the nineteenth century as the Voodoo Queen. Speaking of voodoo, it was a belief and ritual brought to New Orleans by West Indian slaves. The city council tried to suppress this practice in the early 1800s by authorizing tribal dances and music in what was known as Congo Square, which remained a site for African-American social gatherings until the late nineteenth century. It was there that Charles "Buddy" Bolden

Above, a statue of General Beauregard is found at the entrance of City Park where the New Orleans Museum of Art is also located, below.

absorbed some of the Afro-Caribbean beats that are an integral part of the musical idiom he helped create, jazz.

The work of the first jazzman was continued by the greatest jazzman of them all, Louis Armstrong. "Satchmo" was born in New Orleans on July 4, 1900; he went on to turn jazz on its ear by his swing style, a unique melodic rhythm, and improvising, during which he embellished and re-invented what he was playing. His trumpet work has become immortal.

Jazz's definitive ambassador to the world is forever commemorated in New Orleans with the **Louis Armstrong Park**. Opened April 15, 1980 by his widow Lucille, the park is on the former site of Congo Square. It encompasses the New Orleans Theatre for the Performing Arts, where the Orleans Opera Guild holds its classical music and opera season, fall through spring, and the Municipal Auditorium. But in the end, it's jazz that counts in this city, and a statue of Louis Armstrong is meant to keep a watchful eye on a living heritage of New Orleans that he did so much to perpetuate.

Since New Orleans is below sea level, the natives' final resting place must be above ground, as seen by this photo of St. Louis Cemetery Number One, one of the city's oldest burial grounds. Below, Louis Armstrong Park.

LOUIS ARMSTRONG

Old-time steamboats docked along the Mississippi provide a contrast to the skyscapers of the modern city, including the World Trade Center. Right, further up the river the Jackson Brewery and Jackson Square act as a picturesque backdrop for the Natchez steamboat. On the following pages, a streamboat cruise is a must during a visit to New Orleans.

I'VE GOT THE WORLD ON A STRING

The **Mississippi River** adds its own brand of rhythm to New Orleans. Through the ages it has provided the city with the lifeblood and livelihood – immigrants and trade – needed to grow and expand. Deep and swift at this point, the Mississippi splits the area into New Orleans proper and, on the opposite bank, Algiers. The opposite banks are connected by the majestic twin spans of the **Mississippi River Bridge**. New Orleans proper is located in a sharp curve of the river, giving rise to its nickname of "The Crescent City".

A scenic view of the river is obtained below Jackson Square by following the **Moonwalk**, named for a former mayor of the city, Moon Landrieu. At this point you can catch a fascinating

Above, *a night skyline of commercial buildings and hotels (including the Hilton)*, right, *Lee Circle, meeting-place for four major traffic arteries, and a memorial to the Southern hero.*

glimpse into New Orleans' past by looking at the **steamboats** docked along the riverfront. Luxurious paddlewheelers and historic sternwheelers (the latter featuring the paddlewheel at the back, or stern of the boat) with such names as the "Cajun Queen", "Cotton Blossom", "Natchez", "Creole Queen", "Bayou Jean Lafitte" and "Voyageur" provide for short or long sightseeing cruises, or dinner cruises.

The modern reality of New Orleans is that of the second largest **Port** in the United States and the third most productive in the world in terms of commerce. Exports include raw and processed agricultural products, fabricated metals, chemicals, oils, petroleum and petroleum products. Fittingly enough, a significant portion of the city's industry is housed close to the riverfront in the **World Trade Center**, 2 Canal

Above, *the area near the Superdome and the Hyatt hotel,*
right, *the Superdome, which hosts many sporting events.*

Street, along with consular offices of various
nations. A ride in a glass elevator located outside
the 33-story building up to the Observation Deck
allows you a stunning vista, as does a revolving
cocktail lounge two floors above the same deck.
A plethora of skyscapers gives way to the
meeting-place of four main roads, **Lee Circle**,
which honors the memory of Confederate general
Robert E. Lee. From a strategic point atop a
column, the bronze statue of the South's
best-known military man symbolically faces
North. War on a smaller scale is waged
periodically inside the **Louisiana Superdome**, a
gleaming saucer-shaped futuristic building that is
the home of the New Orleans Saints football team
as well as Tulane University's local "Green Wave"
football squad. It is also the site of many Sugar
Bowl and Super Bowl events. One of the largest
buildings of its kind in the world, the Superdome
can seat up to 100,000 people.

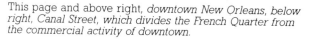
This page and above right, *downtown New Orleans, below right, Canal Street, which divides the French Quarter from the commercial activity of downtown.*

Away from the river at this point, you reach **downtown New Orleans**, the modern city which houses many of the city's 50 commercial banks, retail stores and restaurants. This makes up part of the section the Americans settled in after the city was ceded to the United States in 1803. The center of the American sector was then marked by **Lafayette Square**, named for the French nobleman who did so much to aid the American cause during the Revolutionary War. Nearby on Camp Street a statue of an American hero from the same era, **Benjamin Franklin**, can be found. The base of Franklin's statue is inscribed with a saying from his *Poor Richard's Almanac*: "Save while You Are Young to Spend When You Are Old. One Penny Saved is Better Than Two Pennies Earned".

Going full circle back to the Vieux Carré, you come upon the aforementioned original division between the French Quarter and the rest of New Orleans: **Canal Street**, now a busy boulevard lined with shops and office buildings.

Above left, *Canal Street*, below, and right, *a statue of Benjamin Franklin is located near Lafayette Square.*

The Riverwalk Marketplace offers varied shopping experiences.

EVIDENCE

Beyond the French Quarter, the Moonwalk gives way to the **Riverwalk**, which includes the fun-to-visit **Riverwalk Marketplace**.

Because of its heritage and mercantile character, a true vision of the city must include glimpses of international friendship. A bronze statue or **Joan of Arc**, a gift from four French cities, was presented to New Orleans on behalf of the French government and placed near the International Trade Mart. A statue of **Winston Churchill** is located in British Place in front of the **Hilton Hotel**, the latter a prominent part of the local cityscape. There is even a **Spanish Plaza**, situated next to the World Trade Center, which pays homage to the city's important Spanish link. Not to mention the **Piazza d'Italia**, an open-air temple and a fountain in the shape of the map of Italy, found close to the river.

And, along with the exchange of goods, New Orleans has heavily promoted in recent years an exchange of ideas. This is seen further down the Riverwalk in the shape of the 350,000 square foot **New Orleans Convention Center**, site of the 1988 Republican National Convention. The local economy is boosted by convention activity to the tune of 500 million dollars annually.

Above left, *statues of Winston Churchill and Joan of Arc lend a foreign touch to the city.* Below left, *the Spanish Plaza.* Right, *Piazza d'Italia,* below, *the New Orleans Convention Center.*

Above left, *a close-up of the Hilton hotel and the World Trade Center*, below, *a scene that characterizes activity in the Port of New Orleans.* Above, *the twin spans of the Mississippi River bridge, which links New Orleans to Algiers.*

LADY, BE GOOD

New Orleans is comprised of four parishes (countries): Orleans, Jefferson, St. Bernard and St. Tammany, with an area of 363 square miles (200 of which is land) and a population of over half a million. The two major institutions of higher learning in the city are Tulane and Loyola universities.

Tulane was founded in 1834 as a medical college, and later expanded to include such faculties as business administration (the oldest college of commerce in the U.S.), art, architecture, social sciences, engineering and law (emphasizing the study of the Napoleonic Code, in use only in Louisiana among the U.S. states). **Loyola,** a university administered by the Jesuit order, is the South's largest Catholic university, and has a fine academic reputation.

Both schools are located side by side on **St. Charles Avenue,** one of the few boulevards where a functioning **streetcar** provides public transportation. The New Orleans streetcar, in continuous operation for the past 150 years, is an official Historic Landmark, immortalized in the Tennessee William's play *A Streetcar Named Desire* (in this case, which ran along Desire St.). St. Charles Avenue is also part of the **Garden District,** one of the city's first suburbs, home to lovely historic mansions and thriving oak trees. A

trolley ride, one of the best bargains in town at only 60 cents, permits a tour of the area's elegant architecture, which reflects the Victorian period, and French and Spanish influences, as well as lush vegetation.

Speaking of greenery, the **Audubon Park and Zoological Garden,** named for the famous naturalist who did much of his best work in Louisiana, also boasts a St. Charles Avenue address. The park's 400 acres are a great place for a walk, a picnic, a bike ride, or a golf game.

A visit to New Orleans would hardly be complete without a stop-off at characteristic suburban estates and old-style plantations. The **Longue Vue House and Gardens** is interesting to see, being of ancient design and recent origin. Formal English gardens surround a formal Spanish court; the house itself was built in 1942 according to a

Left, *Tulane University, below, Loyola University, above right, a streetcar crossing Charles Street, and a lovely house in the Garden District, below right, Commander's Place Restaurant and Audubon Park.*

Following pages, above left, *Long Vue Plantation, below left, San Francisco Plantation, above right, Oak Alley Plantation, below right, a delta swamp, which indicates how low-lying the area is.*

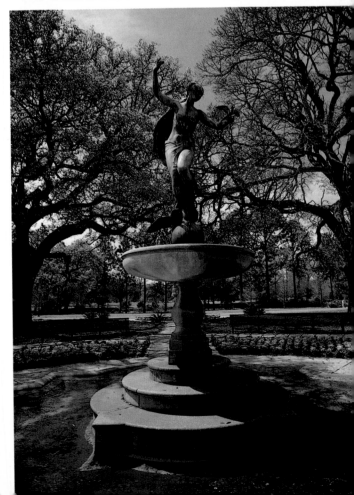

The Mardi Gras is a joyous time in New Orleans, and the city explodes with colorful festivities as you see from the photos on this page and the following pages.

Greek Revival architectural style, and is furnished with eighteenth and nineteenth century French and English antiques. Plantations of noteworthy interest include the **San Francisco, Oak Alley, Houmas House and Nottoway.** Finally, no book on New Orleans would be complete without mentioning the city's world-famous **Mardi Gras,** the "Fat Tuesday" before Ash Wednesday and Lent. In the best French tradition, the two weeks prior to Mardi Gras are filled with parades, both night and day, staged by carnival groups called "krewes". Each group tries to outdo the other in terms of imaginative costume. And, the true nature of New Orleans comes to the fore as it explodes with color and celebration. These two components, after all, are what basically create *jazz*.

INDEX